D0586188

The Gruesome Truth About

The Egyptians

Written by

Jillian Powell

Illustrated by

Matt Buckingham

WAYLAND

First published in 2008 by Wayland

Text copyright © Wayland 2008
Illustration copyright © Matt Buckingham 2008

Wayland
338 Euston Road
London NW1 3BH

Wayland Australia
Level 17/207 Kent Street
Sydney NSW 2000

Senior Editor: Claire Shanahan
Design Manager: Paul Cherrill
Designers: Fiona Grant, Jason Billin
Consultant: Anne Millard
Indexer: Cath Senker

British Library Cataloguing in Publication Data
Powell, Jillian
The gruesome truth about the Egyptians
1. Egypt - Social life and customs to 332 BC-
Juvenile literature
2. Egypt - History to 332 BC - Juvenile literature
I. Title II. The Egyptians 938

ISBN 978 0 7502 5337 6

Printed in China

Wayland is a division of Hachette Children's Books,
an Hachette Livre UK company.
www.hachettelivre.co.uk

Contents

The Extraordinary Egyptians

The ancient Egyptians lived along the banks of the River Nile around 5,000 years ago. Ancient Egypt was a great civilisation that lasted over 3,000 years. It was ruled by kings called **pharaohs** from about 3100 BCE.

The ancient Egyptians were skilled farmers, traders, soldiers, artists, **architects** and **engineers**.

They built magnificent stone pyramids as grand tombs for their pharaohs.

▲ The Egyptians had their own way of writing called **hieroglyphs**.

▲ They learned to **embalm** dead bodies as **mummies** to preserve them.

▲ The pyramids are the oldest of the seven wonders of the ancient world.

The Sun God

The Egyptians worshipped the Sun God in the form of an insect called a **scarab**. Scarabs are dung beetles. The Egyptians thought Khepri rolled the sun across the sky each day, just as scarabs roll dung. They even wore **amulets** and jewels in the shape of scarabs.

▲ Scarabs roll and bury balls of animal dung so that the females can lay their eggs in them.

Those are some things that you probably already know about the Egyptians, but in this book you'll find out the gory and grisly bits that no one ever tells you! Each double page will begin with a well-known FACT, before going on to tell you the gruesome truth about the Egyptians. Look out for these features throughout the book – the answers are on page 32.

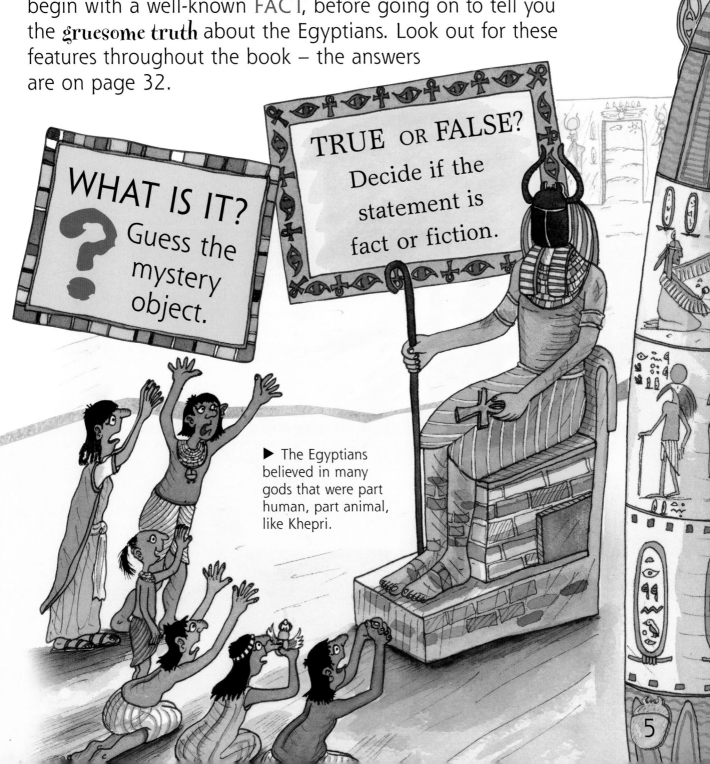

WHAT IS IT?
? Guess the mystery object.

TRUE OR FALSE?
Decide if the statement is fact or fiction.

▶ The Egyptians believed in many gods that were part human, part animal, like Khepri.

5

Powerful Pharaohs

FACT Ancient Egypt was ruled by kings called pharaohs. They were thought of as gods.

Gruesome truth

The pharaohs made Egypt richer by invading other lands and stealing their treasures.

Pharaohs and pygmies

Narmer (about 3150 BCE) beheaded his enemies. He got his name 'the Striking Catfish' from the River Nile fish that gives electric shocks!

▲ One picture of Narmer shows him pulling a prisoner along by a rope through the nose!

Pepi II (about 2278 – 2218 BCE) sent an army to Africa and they brought him back a **pygmy** for his palace. Pepi was so excited by this 'exotic' prisoner that he told his army to check him ten times a night on the boat back home.

Senusret III (1874 – 1855 BCE) fought the Nubians because they kept attacking Egypt. He kidnapped their women, killed their bulls, cut off their water and burned their wheat.

Pharaohs had carvings of themselves made for temples, boasting about how many lions and wild bulls they had killed. On one hunt, Tuthmosis III (1479 – 1425 BCE) killed 120 elephants.

▶ Slaves captured in war were the property of the pharaoh.

Fierce Feet

The soles of a pharaoh's sandals were sometimes decorated with drawings of his enemies, so he could crush them underfoot with every step!

Grave goods

When a pharaoh died, his tomb was filled with everything he would need for the next life – even a toilet!

▲ Sandals decorated with the pharaoh's enemies were found in the tomb of the 'Boy King' Tutankhamun (1334 – 1325 BCE).

▲ The first pharaohs may have had their servants and animals killed and buried with them. Later, they used models.

Pyramids and Peasants

FACT The pyramids are some of the greatest wonders of the ancient world.

Gruesome truth

The pyramids were built by groups of peasants working long hours, with only one day off in ten.

Peasant workers

Most people in ancient Egypt were peasants. They were sold with land and property, and were counted like cattle to show how rich the owner was. When the River Nile flooded farmland, they were sometimes sent to work on building a pyramid for the pharaoh. It took 25,000 men five years to build a pyramid.

Hard labour

Some peasants did back-breaking work in the **quarries**, using hand tools to chip out huge blocks of stone. Others had to haul blocks weighing 60 kilograms across the desert on sledges. Each pyramid took around two million blocks! Men lived in cramped, smelly huts with mud floors and got paid in food and linen.

Some workers got coughs and lung diseases from the sand. Others were stung by scorpions or broke bones in accidents. If they didn't work hard enough, they could be beaten, or even have a finger or toe chopped off.

▼ Men worked in groups of 20, heaving the stones into place.

TRUE OR FALSE?
Pyramid workers went on strike when they didn't get paid.

A Slave's Life

FACT Slaves in ancient Egypt worked as household servants and entertainers, like dancers and acrobats.

Gruesome truth

Some people were sold into slavery by their own families. Others sold themselves to escape debt, or were kidnapped from other countries or captured as prisoners of war.

▲ Sometimes, prisoners of war were **branded** or tattooed to show they were slaves.

Servants and scarecrows

Slaves worked for pharaohs, **nobles** or priests. They were often given as gifts or sold on with land or property. They worked as house servants, on farms or in the mines.

Children were slaves, too. Some had to work as scarecrows in the fields!

▼ Children threw stones or waved their arms around to scare birds away from crops.

Room service

Pharaohs owned thousands of slaves.
In the royal household, each one had
a different job to do.

▲ King Pepi II
(2278 – 2218 BCE)
kept some slaves naked
and covered in honey, so they
kept the flies away from him!

A deadly job

The worst work was being a slave in the gold
and copper mines of Nubia and Sinai.
If the slaves tried to run away, they were
often captured and given a beating.

◀ In the mines and
quarries, water was
rationed and many
slaves died from heat
and exhaustion.

11

Make-up and Wigs

FACT Rich Egyptians wore make-up and wigs.

Gruesome truth

The best wigs were made from human hair. The wig maker had to comb out lice eggs before the wigs could be sold!

Cool heads

Poorer wigs were made from wool or plant fibres. Many people, both men and women, shaved their heads for hygiene and to keep cool. Remedies for grey hair included ox blood, black snake fat, ravens' eggs and rotten donkey liver!

▼ At parties, the rich wore cones of scented wax or animal fat that melted to perfume their wigs.

▲ Mummified lice and lice eggs (nits) have been found on combs from Egyptian tombs.

▲ Pharaohs had their heads shaved because they were priests. They wore false beards made from wool or plant fibres – even female pharaohs!

Childhood plaits

Children had their heads shaved too, except for a plait on the side of the head. It was cut off when they were about 10 years old to show that their childhood was over.

Bathing and beauty

Many people bathed in rivers or canals. They used soap made from ash and clay. Animal fat was used to soften the skin. To get rid of body hair, the ancient Egyptians used a paste made from crushed bird bones, oil and tree gum. They also chewed gum from cedar trees to sweeten their breath.

Men and women wore make-up. It was made from mineral pigments mixed with animal fat. Some Egyptians also had their skin tattooed.

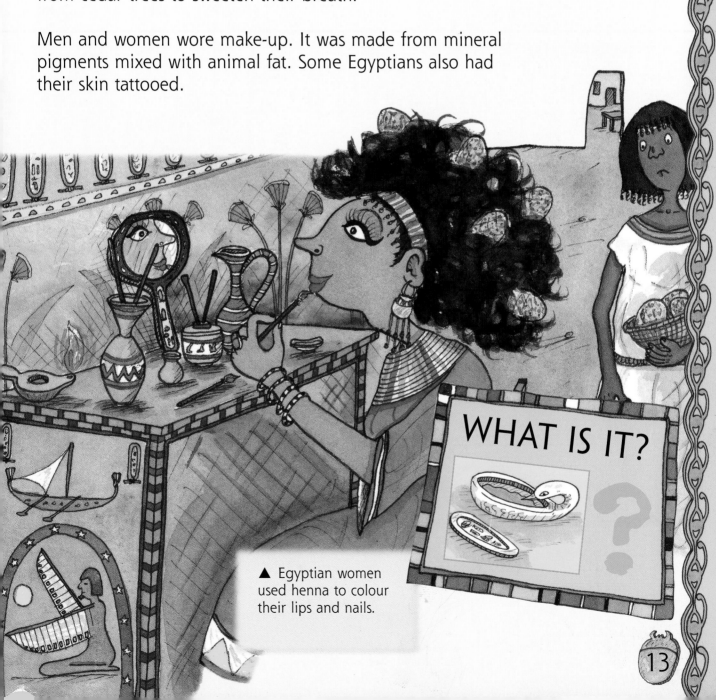

▲ Egyptian women used henna to colour their lips and nails.

WHAT IS IT?

Magic and Medicine

FACT Egyptian doctors trained at special schools. They could stitch wounds and mend broken bones.

Gruesome truth

The poor could not afford doctors. They turned to magic remedies to cure their problems.

Protective amulets

Many Egyptians believed diseases could be caused by enemy spirits. They wore amulets to protect them against injuries and illnesses.

Prayers and remedies

Cures were often combined with magical spells or speeches. For eye problems, the Egyptians poured a mix of honey, red earth and crushed pigs' eyes into the ear, while they said prayers to the gods. Sometimes, images of a god were drawn on to a patient's skin. The patient licked them off to absorb their healing power.

▲ Amulets, often in the form of birds and animals, were carried or worn as jewellery.

► For toothache, a dead mouse was cut in half and placed on the patient's gums.

▲ For baldness, the Egyptians used a paste made from vipers' oil and bats' ears.

▼ One medicine was made from 19 kinds of poo, from fly droppings to ostrich dung!

Mould and maggots

Some doctors' cures did work, though. If a patient had a cut or wound, they cleaned it up with mouldy bread and maggots, or they put raw meat on it and bandages covered in animal fat and honey. The mould and maggots killed the germs.

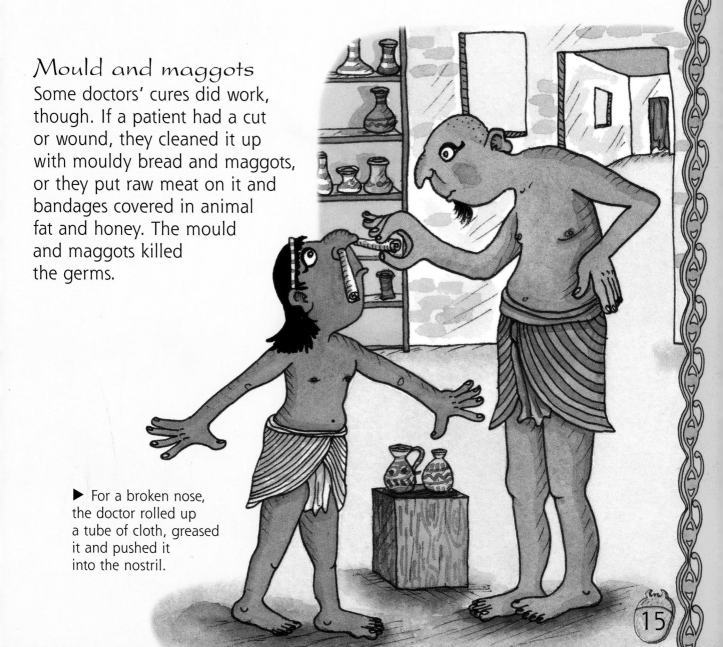

▶ For a broken nose, the doctor rolled up a tube of cloth, greased it and pushed it into the nostril.

15

Hunting and Fishing

FACT The ancient Egyptians were skilled at hunting and fishing.

Gruesome truth

They killed everything from lions, hippos and elephants to hares, hedgehogs and water birds. They killed ostriches for their feathers, and leopards and other big cats for their skins.

Birds and bait

To kill wild birds, they used 'throw sticks'. These were wooden sticks like boomerangs that broke the bird's neck or wing, or knocked it out of the sky. Birds and fish were also caught in nets **baited** with corn or maggots.

▲ Animals were killed to provide meat or materials like ivory and feathers.

To hunt crocodiles, the Egyptians hooked a pig's back and floated it in the river as bait. Then they made a piglet squeal on the riverbank to attract the crocodile. When it went for the pig, they reeled it in.

Hunting chariots

Pharaohs hunted in chariots. Animals were sometimes herded into enclosures for the pharaoh to hunt.

▼ Pharaohs hunted with the help of dogs and tame cheetahs.

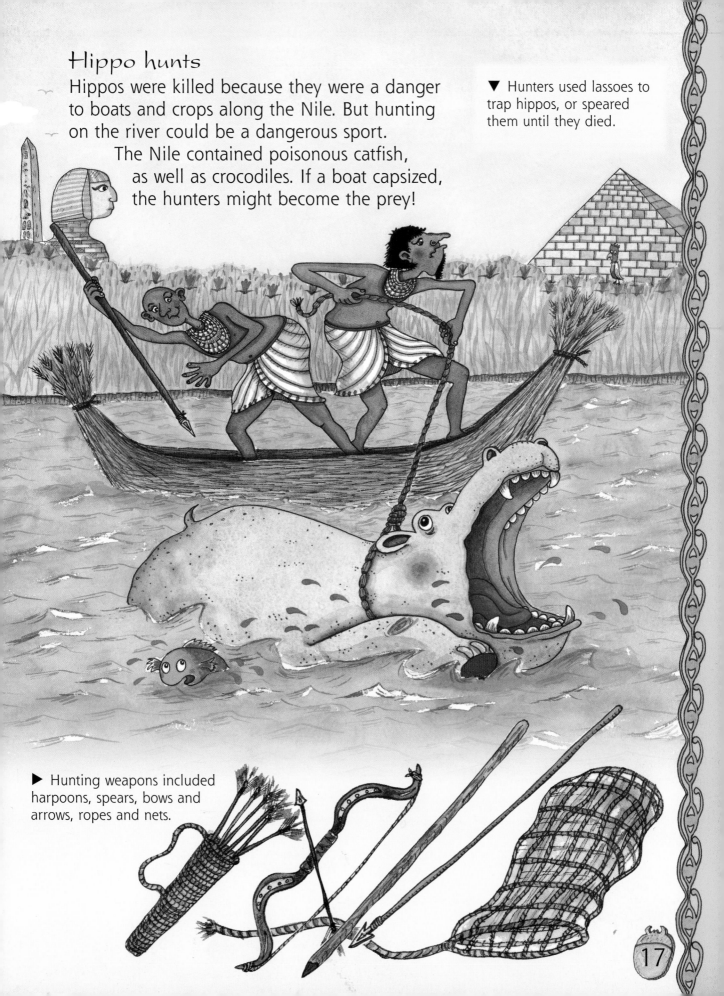

Hippo hunts

Hippos were killed because they were a danger to boats and crops along the Nile. But hunting on the river could be a dangerous sport. The Nile contained poisonous catfish, as well as crocodiles. If a boat capsized, the hunters might become the prey!

▼ Hunters used lassoes to trap hippos, or speared them until they died.

▶ Hunting weapons included harpoons, spears, bows and arrows, ropes and nets.

Gods and Gifts

FACT The Egyptians worshipped gods in temples, in shrines in their houses and along the River Nile.

Gruesome truth

They sacrificed animals and, at one time, enemy leaders of war to please the gods.

Temple tributes
The Egyptians worshipped hundreds of different gods and goddesses. They made offerings of food, drink and other gifts to statues of the gods in their temples.

Animal offerings
Cattle, geese, **antelopes** and **gazelles** were all sacrificed outside temples for the gods. Priests cut the animal's throat, then cut off its head before skinning it.

▲ The gods were even given make-up and mirrors as offerings.

▼ After sacrifice, animal remains were sometimes thrown into the River Nile.

18

Tomb companions

In the days of the first pharaohs, when the king died, his servants, **scribes** and soldiers might be killed and buried with him. They were poisoned, strangled or had their throats cut. His horses, camels, donkeys, dogs and cats were also mummified and put in the tomb.

▼ One early pharaoh's tomb contained over 300 burials – thought to be his servants!

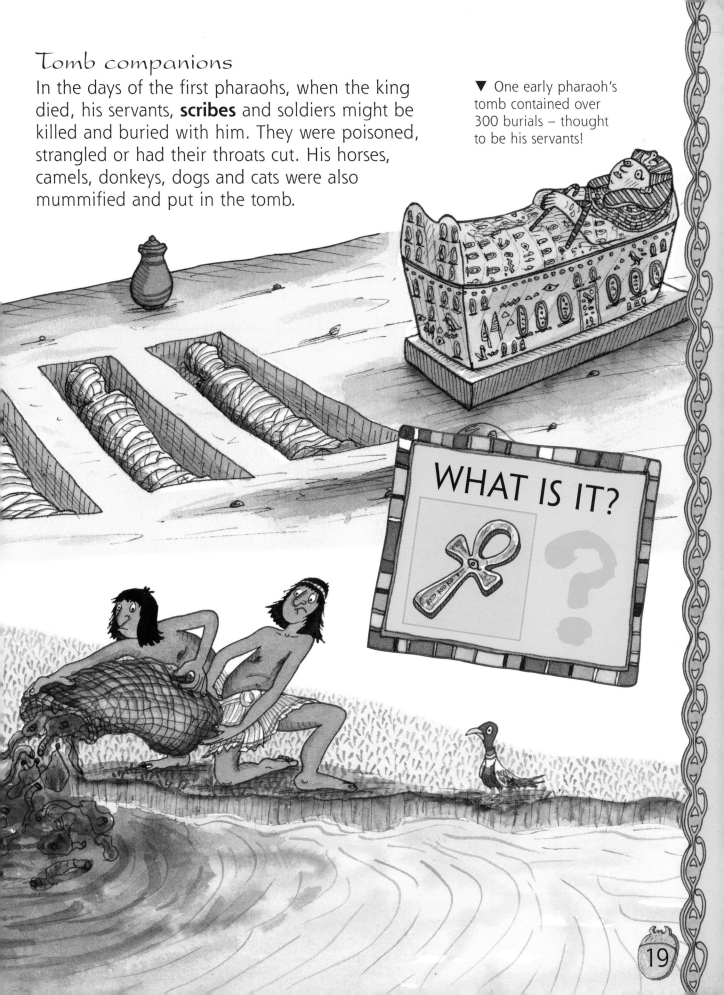

WHAT IS IT?

Water and Worms

FACT The River Nile flooded each year and provided the Egyptians with rich farmland.

Gruesome truth

Nile water contained many kinds of **parasites**. When people waded in the **irrigation** channels, the parasites got into their legs and feet and laid eggs in their blood.

▲ Drinking water contained sewage because toilet waste was thrown into the river, into pits or just out into the street.

Wormy water

The Egyptians used water from the river and from wells for drinking, washing and cooking. The water they drank often contained parasites called guinea worms. People often had stomach upsets because of the dirty water.

Rats and cats

Rats carried fleas that caused diseases. Mice and rats often ate the grain in houses and grain stores. Many people kept cats or rubbed gazelle dung and **cat grease** around the doorways to try to keep rats and mice away.

River bathing

Pharaohs and nobles had bathrooms where slaves poured water over them from behind a screen. But most people bathed in the river or in canals.

▲ The Egyptians shared their homes with many kinds of pests including rats, mice and poisonous snakes.

▼ Bread was so hard and gritty it wore away teeth.

Dismal diets

Bread was an important part of the Egyptian diet. It often contained sand and grit from the millstone that got mixed in with the wheat or barley. Many people drank wine and a lumpy sort of beer, and often got drunk at parties. Wall paintings show party guests being sick, or being carried home after drinking too much.

Criminal Punishments

Gruesome truth

Punishment for crimes included branding, beheading, mutilation and burning alive.

Cruel courts
Law officers took criminals to the pharaoh who decided their punishment in court. This was often a harsh **corporal** punishment, even for small crimes. If a weaver took a day off work, he was punished with 50 lashes of the whip on his back.

▼ If criminals were caught stealing animal hides, they were beaten with a hundred blows until they had five open wounds on their back.

◄ People who avoided taxes could have their nose or ears chopped off.

Grave punishments

Many crimes were punished by death. If anyone stole cattle, he was **impaled** on a sharp stake. His body was lowered slowly onto the stake, until it went right through and killed him. Then his wife and children were forced into slavery.

▲ Killing or injuring a cat was punishable by death, because cats were sacred creatures to the Egyptians.

▼ Grave robbers sometimes bribed the tomb builders or guards.

Deadly decisions

The worst crimes of all were plotting against the pharaoh and grave robbing. Grave robbers didn't just steal tomb treasure – they unwrapped the mummy to get at jewels in the linen! If they were caught, they were tortured and then killed. The pharaoh decided whether they would be drowned, beheaded or burned alive.

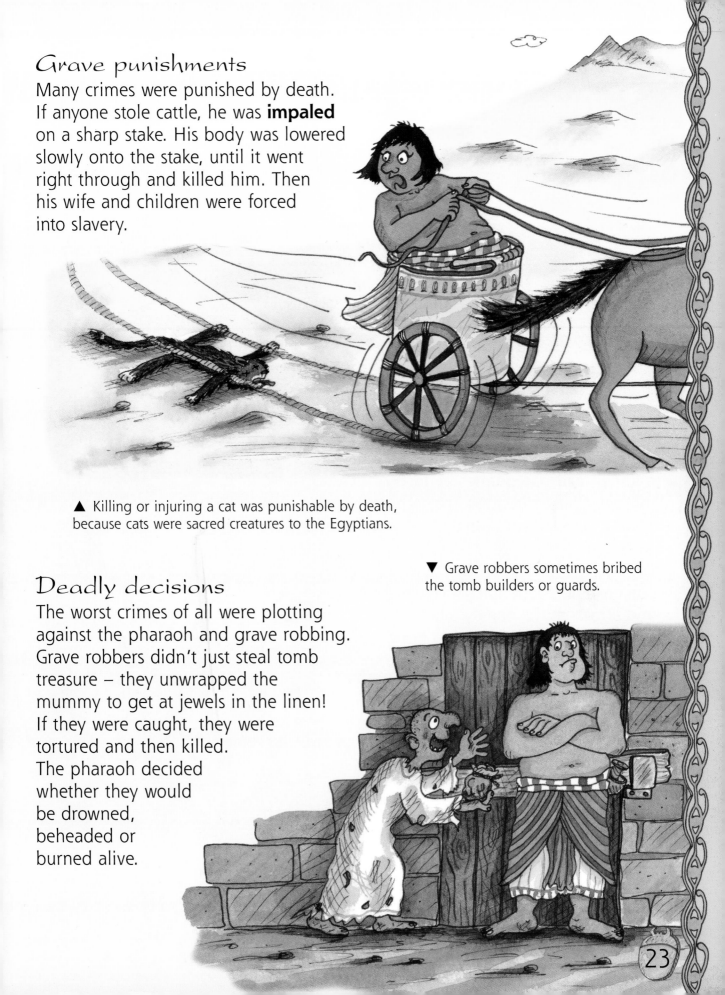

Blood and Battles

FACT The Egyptians had a well-trained army that won land and treasures for the pharaoh.

Gruesome truth

Soldiers chopped off the right hands of their enemies to take back and show how many people they had killed.

Prize parts

They often cut bodies into pieces with axes and collected the body parts as trophies to present to the pharaoh. King Menephta returned with the penises of 1,300 Libyan soldiers after one battle! The remains of the bodies were left for vultures and other **scavengers**.

Chariots and sieges

Some soldiers rode in chariots, firing spears and arrows at the enemy. They used towers and battering rams to fight their way into cities.

They also fought with swords, javelins, knives and throwing sticks. Sometimes, they clubbed their enemies to death with **maces**.

WHAT IS IT?

▶ Carved tablets and wall paintings record battles and victories.

Mummies

FACT The ancient Egyptians learned the art of embalming dead bodies as mummies. They believed that spirits needed a home for the next life.

Gruesome truth

They embalmed mummies in open-air tents because the smell was so bad.

Insides out

First, they laid the dead body on a table and washed it with palm oil to make it smell nicer. Then, an embalmer, called a ripper-up, used a sharp flint knife to cut into the body and remove the insides, leaving only the heart.

◄ The liver, stomach, lungs and guts were washed in palm oil and wrapped in linen, then put into **canopic jars**.

Salt and sawdust

The brain was pulled through the nose using a wire with a hook on the end. The body was put in a bath of **natron** to dry it out. After 40 days, they stuffed it with sawdust, rags or sand and sweet-smelling spices, and sewed it up. They rubbed palm oil into the skin to soften it. Sometimes, they made small cuts in the skin and stuffed them with mud or animal fat to pad out the body.

▼ Embalmers chiselled into the skull through the nose, then pulled out the brain bit by bit.

Spare parts

The Egyptians thought that a body had to be whole to enjoy the next life, so they patched up any wounds with gazelle skin and replaced missing limbs with wooden ones. Embalmers tied on finger and toe nails to stop them dropping off, but sometimes bits of the body fell off or were eaten by jackals.

▲ They put false eyes or onions in the eye sockets and painted the face with make-up.

Linen layers

The Egyptians bandaged the body in about 20 layers of linen. Some people saved up all their lives for their mummy linen. Sometimes, embalmers put amulets between the linen to act as lucky charms and added pads to round out the body shape. Then, they brushed the bandages with a sticky **resin**, which sometimes stuck to the coffin.

▼ There were often several coffins inside each other. Each was decorated with protective spells.

A mask was placed over the head and neck, then the mummy was placed in a coffin.

▼ The ancient Egyptians mummified fish, birds, mice, crocodiles and snakes, as well as cats and dogs.

Mummy pets

The Egyptians thought cats were sacred and important animals. They sold mummies of them outside temples. People bought them to leave as offerings to statues of the gods in temples. When a pharaoh died, the mummies of his pets were buried with him to keep him company in the next life.

▶ Fruit, animal legs and other joints of meat were mummified as food for the dead.

29

Glossary

amulet	A good luck charm worn to keep evil or illness away.
antelope	An animal with hooves and horns, related to deer and goats.
architect	Someone who designs buildings.
baited	To set with food trap.
brand	To mark on the skin by burning.
canopic jar	A jar or urn that contained the organs from embalmed bodies.
cat grease	Grease made from a cat's body fat.
corporal	Affecting the body.
embalm	To preserve a dead body.
engineer	Someone who designs and builds the working parts of engines, machines or buildings.
gazelle	A small type of antelope.
hieroglyphs	A form of writing that uses pictures.
impale	To pierce right through.
irrigation	To water farm crops.
mace	A club that could be made from wood with a stone end.
mummy	A dead body preserved in sand or ice or by embalming.
noble	Someone from a rich or important family.
natron	A kind of salt crystal.
parasite	A creature that lives on a host animal.
pharaoh	An ancient Egyptian king or queen.
pygmy	A race of very small people from Africa.
quarry	A deep pit for digging stone.
resin	A sticky tree gum.
scarab	A kind of beetle.
scavenger	An animal that feeds on dead animals.
scribe	A writer or scholar.

Further Information

Books

Ancient Egypt (History Beneath Your Feet),
by Jane Shuter, Wayland 2008

The Awesome Egyptians (Horrible Histories),
by Terry Deary, Peter Hepplewhite, and
Rebecca Ferrara, Scholastic Hippo 1993

The Awful Egyptians (Horrible Histories),
by Terry Deary, Scholastic Hippo 2006

Men, Women and Children in Ancient Egypt,
by Jane Bingham, Wayland 2007

You Wouldn't Want to Be an Egyptian Mummy,
by David Stewart, Wayland 2000

Websites

www.ancientegypt.co.uk
www.bbc.co.uk/history/ancient/
egyptians
www.historyforkids.org/learn/egypt
www.nms.ac.uk/education/egyptian

Places to visit

The Ancient Egypt Gallery, Leicester
The British Museum, London
The National Museums, Edinburgh,
Scotland

 # Illustrator Note

The ancient Egyptians have always
fascinated me from when I first learned
about them at school. Their amazing
buildings, artwork and religion stand
as a testament to time for us all to see.
However, time has not forgotten the other
side of Egyptian life, the ghastly, grisly bits
not normally told. Through illustrating this
book, I have learned that there are some
terribly gruesome truths about the
Egyptians, too.

Matt Buckingham

Index

Answers

Page 9 True or false? True. The first ever workers' strike was by peasants working on a pyramid for Ramses III (1184 – 1153 BCE).

Page 13 What is it? A face cream pot in the shape of a mother duck.

Page 19 What is it? An ankh, the ancient Egyptian symbol of life, which only gods and pharaohs were allowed to carry.

Page 24 What is it? Medals shaped like gold flies were awarded for bravery in battle.